AF621196

Pages and pages of animals we see in the zoo to colour! Get this handy, bag-shaped colouring book for your little one. This easy-to-carry book with cute, black-and-white illustrations to colour is the perfect companion for every preschooler.

- Will keep children occupied for hours
- Fun way for children to learn about colours and colouring
- Ideal book to improve children's motor skills and encourage creativity

COLOURMANIA

Scan Now!

Children | Colouring US$ 4.95

978-81-319-3743-3

PEGASUS

www.pegasusforkids.com

₹90